I AM MY BELOVED'S

I Am My Beloved's

CHRISTIAN DEVOTIONALS FOR THE BRIDE TO BE

BY

Amy Hayes

MADISON STREET
PUBLISHING

I Am My Beloved's: Christian Devotionals for the Bride to Be

Copyright © 2012–2014 by Amy Hayes

Published by Madison Street Publishing, Oregon City, Oregon

Cover and Interior design by Masha Shubin
Cover Image: "Wedding" © Eminavn. BigStockPhoto.com
Author photo by Miwaza Jemimah

ISBN 978-0-9836719-7-8

1 3 5 7 9 10 8 6 4 2

This book is dedicated to three women without whom I would have nothing to say:

Mom, for the example
Lorna, for the inspiration
Nancy Wilson, for words of wisdom

Contents

Author's Preface ix

Foreword...xi

A New Name 1

A Time of Preparation.. 9

Bridezilla 13

In Everything, Give Thanks! 19

A Gracious Woman of Valor 25

Capturing a Vision... 33

Girlfriends 39

Honoring Marriage 45

Gracious Beauty.. 51

Memory Keeper 55

Building Your Storehouse 61

Rejoicing in the Lord 71

Giving Good Gifts to Your Groom 77

Say Thank You.. 87

Author's Preface

THIS BRIDAL DEVOTIONAL IS EXCERPTED FROM THE LARGER work *All Things Are Ready: A Bride's Complete Christian Wedding Planner* (Doorposts Publishing, 2012).* I set out to write this wedding planner because everything on the market seemed to have the wrong focus. What to do two years before your wedding; what to do eighteen months ahead, etc. Nothing for the bride who is less concerned about dates than she is about glorifying God in her wedding day. So, I culled together various notes and resources from my years of planning and coordinating weddings and wrote my own planner. My goal is to encourage brides to use this special time in their lives to work toward the kind of wife they hope to be, to be a blessing to those around them, and above all, to glorify God throughout the period of life we call *engagement*.

---

* The full text of *All Things Are Ready: A Bride's Complete Christian Wedding Planner* can be purchased from Doorposts at www.Doorposts.com. The companion website to these books is found at www.weddingchristian.com.

With this end in view, I wrote a small devotional for each chapter of the wedding planner. These notes, addressed just to the bride, center on keeping your perspective and focus during the tumultuous weeks of wedding planning. How will you exhibit the fruit of the Spirit and Christlikeness in your bride-hood? How can you not lose heart or lose your mind in the midst of wedding planning stress? What good things can you accomplish while creating your dream wedding? Thoughts on these questions and more are given for the bride to meditate on as she tries on dresses and picks out colors.

These bridal devotions are reproduced here in a separate format for those brides who may not need an entire wedding planner, but would still be glad to pause for a moment now and then to be refreshed and encouraged in graciousness and godliness as they enjoy their time as a bride. May you find joy and strength for your bridal journey in these few words, and may God bless and keep you as you approach your wedding day.

Amy Hayes

Foreword

MY HUSBAND HAS OFFICIATED AT MORE WEDDINGS than we have kept track of, but I believe last time his secretary counted, and throwing in the ones since then, it was closing in on a hundred. I've attended most of those weddings, as well as many of the rehearsals and rehearsal dinners. I've even played the part of "go girl" many times. (That's what we call the person who stands at the door and tells the bridesmaids, "Go!") So I guess you could say, I've seen it all when it comes to Christian weddings.

I've also seen a great need for something like this wonderful Christian Wedding Planner that Amy Hayes has so carefully assembled. Our modern secular culture has imitated the form of a Christian wedding service but has lost its perspective on what a wedding is really for. The Christian paradigm is simple and straightforward: a wedding is a beautiful and joyful celebration of the covenant of marriage, and the whole event is designed to glorify God and celebrate His goodness to us creatures.

The Christian bride has a tremendous advantage because she knows her wedding is a doorway and the house is the marriage. Her priorities are different; she's not trying to create a spectacle, but adorn a gracious ceremony. But she still needs a boat-load of help to pull this thing off, and help has arrived!

This wedding planner walks the bride through all the preparations and keeps her focused on the important things, like staying in fellowship with her groom and her parents. It's full of suggestions and ideas, with a strict time-line to keep the bride on task. I know I will recommend this helpful guide to all those planning weddings, and I think we'll keep one in the church office for check out.

Amy Hayes has been a wedding coordinator long enough to know that a bride needs to feel relaxed on the big day, and the only way that can happen is if she knows everything is ready. I remember a wedding where the bride was so exhausted from last-minute preparations that we thought she was going to collapse. This book will help get the bride down the aisle beautifully and calmly. I often tell the bride to fasten her eyes on her groom as she makes the long trek down the aisle on her father's arm. And I remind her of a line from an old hymn: "The bride eyes not her garment, but her dear bridegroom's face."

Nancy Wilson

I AM MY BELOVED'S

A New Name

"I am my beloved's and my beloved is mine."

(SONG OF SONGS 6:3)

THE GLORY OF A WEDDING IS TWO PEOPLE BECOMING ONE in Christ. A new family. New identities taken as new names are bestowed—Husband and Wife. Partners who will carry forth His work better as one than as two halves. Marriage is a beautiful picture of love, cherishing, submitting, and working which reflects the relationship of Christ and His Church. It is a marvelous mystery and one of the greatest joys of our journey through life in God's world.

Even now, before you are named Wife, you have taken on a new name, identity, and work. **Your name now is Bride.** The question is: how will you wear this name? Will you be the Bride who is making herself ready for the Bridegroom (Revelation 19:7-8, Esther

2:12-13)? Or will a self-seeking attitude bring confusion and disorder to your wedding planning (James 3:16)?

The bride is usually considered the center of the wedding preparations. This means you will receive much of the attention, glory, and blessings. It also means you set the tone. Just as a woman creates the atmosphere of a home for good or ill (Proverbs 12:4, 14:1, 18:22, 19:13-14, 21:9, 19, 25:24, 27:15, 31:10), the bride creates the tone of an engagement. How you think, act, speak, and work during the next weeks and months will determine whether your engagement is a time of joy and anticipation or stress and frustration. How will you wear the name of Bride?

Consider the weeks that lie before you as an opportunity. What can you do during your time as "Bride" to be a blessing? There are many people surrounding you during engagement that you can bless with love, joy, peace, patience, kindness, goodness, gentleness, and self-control. Consider your husband-to-be, mother, mother-in-law, father, maid-of-honor, bridesmaids, friends, your groom's friends—the list could go on. For many of these participants, your attitude toward them will determine their experience of your wedding. Bestow blessings upon them.

One way to bless those around you is to **share your joy.** Most couples will naturally be pretty wrapped up in only each other during their engagement. It will bless your friends and family, however, if you take time to bring them into your plans, conversations, and activities. Give liberally of your time and attention. Enjoy their excitement over your happiness. Your friends and family will want to be a part of what is going on with you and be reassured that they still have a place in your life. Take time to notice what is happening in their lives. Be careful not to fall out of all other relationships as you focus on your relationship with your fiancé.

A bride can also be a blessing by **practicing the good habits of a godly wife now**. Ward off the many temptations incumbent in being a bride by actively choosing to love your groom in your words, actions, thoughts, and priorities. It is very easy as a bride to unintentionally fall into unlovely habits. Avoiding this requires actively pursuing the *good* habits you wish to have as a wife. Remember to put your groom's desires before yours in the details of the wedding, seek out ways to include and enjoy his family members in your plans, take time to put aside planning and just focus on giving love and attention to him, and spend time praying and preparing for your coming role as wife. Such positive actions will help keep you from sin and prepare you to be a blessing to your husband when you exchange "Bride" for "Wife." Habits are hard to break for good or ill. Use your engagement period to form good habits.

Also keep in mind that your groom may or may not have as much time as you to spend on the wedding.

Be gracious and understanding of his time constraints and energy level. Give time to one another that doesn't involve the wedding. If possible, consider taking one night a week as a date-night during which no wedding plans are discussed. Go out and enjoy one another's company. Talk about his week at work and your future together. Tell him what you appreciate about him. This may seem obvious; however, as the busyness and stress of the wedding builds, you may find yourself forgetting to do these simple things. As far as is possible with you, do not let the wedding overshadow the marriage. Put your fiancé and your relationship with him first.

Aside from the relationship with your groom, two of the people you can most bless during your time as a bride are **your parents**. This can be a particularly difficult transition for parents. While you are excited to start a new life, they are anticipating letting you go and the many changes that will bring. This will be even more true if you have been living at home with them up to your wedding day. Little attentions towards your parents will make your time as a bride especially sweet to them as well as you.

Typically, **Mom** will be heavily involved in the wedding plans and trying to spend as much time with you as possible before you marry. Do your best to welcome the extra involvement and be grateful for her help. Be sensitive to your mom's stress level and gracious as you work through problems with the wedding plans or differences of opinion on wedding decisions.

Keep in mind that she may have been dreaming of this day even longer than you have! Most moms will feel particularly blessed by a daughter who makes an effort to spend time together before the wedding. Go on a mother-daughter date. Ask your mom's advice on your coming marriage. Be creative in finding ways to show your appreciation for all she has done to prepare you to be a wife. Let her know that you want her to be a part of your special day *and* new life.

Dad is often expected to stay in the background and just write checks. Many dads, however, would love to have their opinions requested and considered. Does he have any ideas or wishes for how his money is spent? His helpful input may extend beyond who you should marry, if only you'd ask him!

Dad also probably has a lot to work through at the thought of *giving away* his daughter. Continuing to show deference and affection for your father as you prepare to leave his home and leadership will strengthen your relationship and bless him. What thoughtful actions can you take towards your father when you are spending your final weeks as Daddy's girl? He will appreciate the attention just as much as Mom.

As you walk through this wedding process, it will help you navigate possible pit-falls if you make it your mission from the beginning to put on the self-sacrificial

mind of Christ in your attitudes and responses to the various situations that will arise during the wedding preparations (Philippians 2:2-16). Hold your plans loosely. Realize that some things just won't work out. Consider others' plans, needs, and expectations as you approach various decisions and especially disagreements that may arise. Take a moment's pause before responding to every situation. Check your attitude. Begin your wedding planning process with a commitment to put on the mind of Christ, who laid down His life for others.

Lastly, **enjoy this time!** That also may seem a little obvious. Sometimes, though, when we get carried away with the busyness of life we forget to step back and take joy in the process. Enjoy the memories you are making with your mom, your girlfriends, your fiancé, and your families. It may be cliché, but stopping to smell the roses is valuable advice. Planning the wedding may be a bit of a blur, but try and pause once in a while to enjoy your moments. If nothing else, take lots of pictures so you can look back and enjoy them later! Ecclesiastes tells us there is nothing better than to eat, drink, and enjoy the fruit of our labor. Be sure in the midst of all your wedding labors to take a few minutes to enjoy them.

Each of the devotionals in this book is designed to encourage you in your journey to wifehood. Each contains a little something to meditate on in the midst of your plans, to help you focus on becoming a wife and finding joy along the way. I pray you will find these encouraging. May they help you relax, enjoy your wedding planning, and *be* a blessing and *find* blessing in it all.

A Time of Preparation

READY? SET. GO! FROM THE MOMENT HE PUTS THAT engagement ring on your finger, you've probably been in high gear wedding mode. You have a thousand things to think about at once, and a million people to talk to, and about a gallon of adrenaline pumping through your system. In the midst of this flurry of wedding preparations, I encourage you to take time to prepare *yourself*.

As I mentioned in the last chapter, you have taken on a new name—Bride. Naming bestows identity and with a new identity comes a new mission to fulfill. Bride may be a short-lived name, but it is a particular calling to lay hold of. In Scripture, a bride is often portrayed as a woman who is preparing herself. Revelation 19 describes Christ's Bride, the Church, as one who makes herself ready for the marriage supper of the lamb. In Esther, the potential brides of King Ahasuerus spent a year in preparations before they came before the king.

Now is your time of preparation before you walk the aisle towards your own Prince Charming.

The bridal preparations described by Scripture are not what you might think. If your pastor's wife told you the Bible encourages you to prepare to be a glorious bride, what would you suppose she meant? Practices such as studying the Word as it speaks to wives, praying for your future husband, and applying good relationship skills would likely spring to mind. While all these are true and good considerations, they are not the bridal preparations described in the passages mentioned above. In their twelve months of apportioned bridal preparations, the young women of Esther spent, "six months with oil of myrrh, and six months with perfumes and preparations for beautifying women." The Bride of Christ is described as arraying herself in fine linens, costly jewels, and beautiful ornaments (Isaiah 49:18, 61:10; Joel 2:16; Revelation 21:2). In Ezekiel 16, when the Lord is preparing his Bride, Israel, He covers her with jewels, costly oils, and fine clothes.

Devoting time and great expense to the adornment of a bride doesn't seem to be discouraged at all in Scripture. Rather, such attention to beauty appears to be promoted as one of her main concerns. A bride's beauty is a reflection of the perfect and glorious Bride of Christ. I Corinthians 11:7 tells us that women are the glory of men. Being the most beautifully splendid bride you can be is a glory both to God and to the man God has given you to marry.

Given this liberty and even encouragement to expend time and money on personal beauty and adornment, what special measures can you take to be a glorious bride on your upcoming wedding day? What preparations would best aid your skin, hair, nails, clothing, and appearance to be at its most beautiful? Consider making room in your budget for beauty products you might not normally indulge in. Would you enjoy and benefit from special skin care products, high quality cosmetics, or salon treatments such as a facial or manicure? Make time to take care of yourself so that you can look your best. Get plenty of rest and nourishment, stay hydrated, find ways to do things that help you relax and de-stress. A relaxed and happy bride is a more beautiful bride. Perhaps plan to spend the extra money and hire a hairdresser to do your hair in a more elaborate style for the wedding day, or have your makeup done at a salon. Adorn yourself with special clothing from the skin out for your wedding day and beautiful jewelry that complements your attire. Wear that which will make you feel beautiful and feminine. If you feel beautiful and happy, you will radiate beauty.

Many of these things may seem like expensive luxuries, but consider what six months of costly oils and perfumes would have meant in biblical times! What we spend time and money on, we value. The extra expense and time you give to beauty preparations for your wedding day will remind you that you are being prepared to be a wife. You value that role and are willing to go to great cost to be a bride that is glorious for her bridegroom. Adorning yourself for your groom will carry over into other ways of being your best for him. Beauty is a virtue, just as patience and humility, when it adorns a faithful woman of God. Be a beautiful bride.

Bridezilla

IN THE FIRST CHAPTER, YOU WERE CHALLENGED TO ANSWER the question, "How will you wear the name of Bride?" We briefly considered a few positive ways you can choose to wear your bride-hood well. While you are still early in the season of being a bride, I'd like to take a moment to consider the *other* side of Bride.

No one sets out to be the kind of bride shown on reality TV shows. You know, the one throwing a fit in the dressing room or screaming at all her friends because they won't agree on which color to wear. Well, maybe you could fake it if they were going to pay you a fortune to do so for television! But in reality we all hope we would never behave in such outlandish fashion.

You might be surprised, though, at some of the things a normal, sweet Christian girl will say and do when she becomes a bride. There's just something about all the expectations, dreams, decisions, nerves and hormones that seem to transform an otherwise perfectly lovely girl into Bridezilla. Here's the trouble.

From the moment when you first watched Cinderella as a little girl, you've been dreaming about how beautiful you will be when your Prince Charming sweeps you away. Everyone will call you The Fairest of Them All, all your dreams will come true and everything will be just as perfect as you imagined it. For the past couple of decades this Disneyfied version of wedding bliss has been fed and nurtured by every female in your life. You dream of what kind of flowers you'll choose, what the church will look like, and what color the bridesmaids will wear. Your girlfriends giggle over it with you at slumber parties. Your mother has tenderly shown you her grandmother's wedding album and told you one day you'll get to wear her wedding tiara. You've daydreamed and planned and hoped and dreamed.

Now, finally, it's your turn. It's your time to choose colors and try on dresses. You are the guest of honor at all the parties, and your wedding is the topic of conversation in the church foyer each Sunday. It's your turn to be Cinderella and have everything turn out just the way you imagined.

Only, one morning, in the midst of creating this fairy tale wedding, you wake up and realize you forgot to secure a Fairy Godmother. Who is going to wave a wand and produce everything you've imagined, exactly as you've imagined it? What happens when other people don't share your vision of how the wedding should, yes *must*, be?

This is when a lovely, happy bride transforms into an overemotional, complaining, demanding, picky, snappish basket-case full of hurt feelings and bad attitudes. Things are just not turning out the way you planned. No one is cooperating. Everyone has an opinion and you don't want to hear any of them. You just want things done the way you want. You're the bride and this is your wedding, darn it!

Somehow in our American wedding culture there has arisen a sense of entitlement for brides. The bride always gets her way and her will is law. Have you ever seen a *Bride's* magazine with a picture of the groom on the cover? It is easy to be sucked into this mindset and let it turn you into the dreaded Bridezilla.

So, what is the antidote to all this madness? Actually, it's rather simple. Remembering just one thing throughout your engagement will keep you from all of these pitfalls. "Greater love hath no man than this, than he lay down his life for his friends" (John 15:13).

Wear these words as a talisman against all your natural temptations to become so wrapped up in your dreams that you forget to act like a Christian during your engagement. Lay it down. Lay down your life. Lay down your plans, your hopes, your dreams for the sake of others. Consider others more important than yourself (Philippians 2:2-15). Consider others' feelings, their hopes and dreams for the wedding, their needs and desires. A wedding does not exempt you from putting on love, joy, peace, patience, kindness, goodness, faithfulness, gentleness and self-control for the length of your engagement.

Are you frustrated because your bridesmaid refuses to wear the strapless dress you've chosen? Lay it down. Be considerate of another's conscience and refuse to label her as "difficult."

Are you disappointed that your mother didn't offer you Grandma's tiara for your wedding veil? Lay it down. Save yourself from carrying around a hurt that will make you bitter.

Is the church you dreamed of too expensive? Lay it down. Don't cause your parents to give up their life savings to keep you happy.

Does your fiancé disagree about the music for the processional? Lay it down. Don't be a bride who thinks the groom's job is to remain silent.

Consider what your groom, mother, mother-in-law, and girlfriends have each individually hoped and dreamed for this wedding day. Don't place your desires above any of them simply because you are The Bride.

Perhaps most importantly, lay down your life for your groom. At the risk of sounding like a broken record, I will say again, *now* is the time to begin building your coming marriage. In the next few weeks your actions may fill your husband-to-be with joyful anticipation at the kind of woman he is gaining as a wife. Alternatively, you could create much to overcome as you pass from Bride to Wife. Self-centeredness, being too busy to notice your fiancé's interests and needs, complaining about what *his* mother wants for *your* wedding or how much everyone expects from you, and acting dismissive of his desires for the wedding are all common failings of brides. Such habits often carry over into marriage. In the midst of wedding preparations, it can be quite easy to forget that the point of all this fuss is not to have a *wedding* but to *be married*. The bride of the Song of Songs calls out, "I am my beloved's and my beloved is mine!" Will your beloved still consider it a blessing that you are his by the time you reach your wedding day? Or will weeks of wedding arguments, tantrums, and tear-fests leave him wondering what he has gotten himself into?

Now, of course, the grim picture I draw is an exaggeration. Only the worst example of a bride will do all of this. However, it's good to keep in mind those things you wish to avoid. Most of us are not as wonderful as we would like to think, and we are usually much closer to ugly than we would like to admit. Pause for a few moments of serious self-evaluation every so often during this engagement, and make sure you are acting now as the kind of wife you hope to be.

Love your neighbor as yourself. Lay down your life for your loved ones during your engagement. Doing so will bring greater joy and beauty to your wedding day than any amount of perfect decorations or gorgeous dresses could ever accomplish.

In Everything, Give Thanks!

But above all this, put on love, which is the bond of perfection.
And let the peace of God rule in your hearts, to which
also you were called in one body; and be thankful.

(COLOSSIANS 3:14-15, EMPHASIS ADDED)

WHAT A JOYFUL BLESSING TO BE IN LOVE AND GETTING married. The intensity of love, excitement, and anticipation during engagement is a unique, wonderful, exhilarating, exhausting thing. Enjoy this time. There's really nothing quite like it. Most couples are so thankful when the wedding day arrives because the stress and intensity of engaged life is so exhausting! They are ready to get on with married life. However, they also look back on engaged life as a special kind of new love and excitement. It is glorious, for a season.

Savor this season of your love. Let thanksgiving be the song you sing as your heart overflows with joy.

Weddings remind us of fairy tales. The term "Fairytale Wedding" is so common that it has become cliché in wedding product advertising. In a fairytale world, the hero or heroine is often protected by some special charm. This charm, whether it be a fairy godmother's gift or a cloak of invisibility, magically protects the bearer from harm in situations full of danger and ominous possibility. How often when we are grown and have left Never-Never-Land behind do we still wish for a little fairy-dust to allow us to fly away from looming troubles? Well, when it comes to the multitude of dangerous possibilities present in the money-matters of wedding planning, God has provided just the charm you need: **"In everything, give thanks"** (1 Thessalonians 5:18).

Money is hard. There is seldom enough. Everything you want for the wedding will cost more than you hoped or imagined it could. There are many monetary temptations. "Just buy the perfect dress. It's The One for you. You can just charge this one thing for now and worry about paying for it after the wedding when you have fewer things on your plate."

Money can be a stumbling block. "I'm so sorry. I thought we were going to have this perfect wedding like we talked about, but my parents just aren't giving me as much as I thought," or, "I guess we can't have

20

that church we both wanted, Mom and Dad are only giving us $X for the wedding and I thought it would be $Y because that's what they gave Jane for hers." Money is a world of opportunity for the devil and his little minions of greed, envy, bitterness, and dissatisfaction.

Money is also a blessing. It is a tool God gives us to create beauty and blessing. It allows us to share the joy of our marriage with our friends and families and bless them in our rejoicing. It is a gift to be thankful for. It is a way for those providing money for the wedding to show their love and happiness for you. Used positively when creating a wedding, money can be a means of grace toward others and an instrument for bringing glory to God.

Money affects relationships. All the discussions, decisions, and differences regarding what is spent on the wedding can become one of the greatest sources of broken relationship and stress in planning a wedding. Not only your wedding plans, but the marriage you are creating can be affected by these struggles. Many wedding-budget frustrations have gone on to become marital grudges or habits that create stumbling blocks for years to come. Money is never really the problem. Your heart attitude towards money determines its effect on your wedding, relationships, and spirit.

Your heart, your relationships, and ultimately, your wedding will be rescued from every distress presented by the wedding budget when you wrap them all in a spirit of thankfulness. God is no fairy godmother. His gift of thankfulness is greater protection from wedding-budget woes than any charm. Start with the Giver of the good gift of money. Thank God for providing all you need to have just the right wedding by whatever means it has come to you. Thank your parents for working hard to have enough to give you a wedding, if that is your situation. Thank your groom for diligently preparing for marriage and working to provide for the new family you are creating. Whatever your wedding budget is, every penny of it is God's provision for you. It is just enough, because it is what He has given you, and all of His gifts are good. Be thankful for the blessing of a God who provides.

A spirit of thanksgiving as you take the money you have available and use it wisely on your wedding will enable you to find joy where others find stress. If you can be thankful no matter how little or much your parents can afford or *choose* to spend on your wedding, then there is no opportunity for bitterness to creep in. When you are satisfied with how much you have to spend on the wedding and don't spend a dime more, your future life together will be protected from the bondage of debt. Thankfulness for what you are able to get for the amount of money you have will guard you from looking back at what you "could have had" if there was "just a little more" money.

Cultivate an attitude of thanksgiving that finds joy

where others find frustration. Be the bride who says, "I'm just so grateful to be marrying you, I don't care where the wedding is held!" Be so pleased to have parents who are happy for you that you wouldn't dream of complaining to your friends or fiancé about how little Dad and Mom are contributing to the wedding budget. Trust that God's provision is just right so that you do not stray down the paths of dissatisfaction. A satisfied heart doesn't dwell with longing on the dress you "really wanted" because it delights in the dress you could afford. Thankfulness is a protective cover from regret, discontent, bitterness, and worry. Thankfulness fills you with pleasure, delight, and peace.

A spirit of thankfulness turns every potential stumbling block into an opportunity for good. Gratitude towards those providing money for your wedding will allow that money spent to be a bond of love between them and you. Working together to use the money available in the best way possible can be a joyful, relationship-building victory for you and your fiancé. Thankfulness poured out on the many people serving you by helping with your wedding, monetarily or otherwise, will give joy to the work they are doing. A grateful heart will be able to see opportunities for using your wedding money to bless others. Giving thanks in all the aspects of your wedding will cause it to be glorifying to God in its grandeur or its simplicity.

Choose thankfulness and you will be choosing joy.

Joy and thanksgiving create peace. Debt, envy, bitterness, and dissatisfaction create stress and lead to death—death of everyone's joy. Choose joy. Be thankful.

A Gracious
Woman of Valor

THROUGHOUT THESE BRIDAL DEVOTIONALS, YOU WILL read many encouragements not to be demanding about what you want for the wedding. Don't be Bridezilla; do be thankful. These encouragements to godly character as a bride should not lead you to conclude that it is somehow wrong to do your best to make all your wedding dreams come true. God likes giving His children good gifts. He loves it when our dreams come true. It is the *manner* in which you make them come true that is of concern and has been discussed. Knowing what you want and creatively bringing that to fruition is a good and godly ability. The reverse trouble of the demanding bride is the bride who has no idea how to create the wedding she wants. She may not even know what she wants. Being wishy-washy and indecisive can make you just as much of a chore for others as being a selfish monster.

The women of Scripture are strong women. Sarah left home for a travelling life, not knowing where home would ever be again. Mary bore the Savior in the face of a ruined reputation with her friends and family who probably found it hard to believe her claim to a virgin birth. People were not always happy with them; they often had to make hard decisions. Proverbs 31 commends to us a woman who knows what she is about and takes on her life confidently. "Virtuous wife" in Proverbs 31:10 can be translated "woman of valor." It conveys might, strength, power, and ableness, according to the *Theological Wordbook of the Old Testament*. This is the kind of woman every bride should strive to be.

Mighty. Ready to work hard, pursue and accomplish the tasks at hand, physically able to do all that is required to keep up with the wedding schedule and workload.

Strong. Emotionally steadfast and able to be gracious to others' input and ideas without becoming incapacitated for wedding planning by a need to keep everyone happy.

Powerful. A woman who can make things happen.

Able. Well informed about her options and competent to make choices and put a plan into action.

This woman of valor makes for a bride who is a joy to serve and easy to please. She is a blessing to all those working on her wedding. There are many people who will each have a separate role to play in your wedding. To serve you well and cheerfully, they need to know what is expected of them and what you want for your wedding. When you are unable to provide this because you find yourself hampered by indecision or crippled by a fear of regretting every choice, it makes everyone's work more difficult. However, if you are able to come up with a plan and direct those helping you to put it into action, everyone will find joy in serving you and find you easy to please. When you avoid looking back on the decisions you've made with worry and regret, it frees those implementing your decisions to joyfully give you their best. Bless those who are helping you with the wedding by being that mighty woman who knows what she is about and moves forward confidently.

There are a thousand different ways to "do" a wedding. Choose one you think you and your fiancé will be happy with and then also choose to be happy with it! A woman of might and ableness approaches her options carefully and wisely and then *chooses*. Once she has chosen, she moves forward without backward glances or regret. Do not allow yourself to constantly wonder if you really would have been happier with that "other" thing. Everyone will just end up wishing you were a pillar of salt! Many emotional struggles like regret are solved by giving up our decisions to God and trusting His sovereign hand in our work. We must strive for wisdom and then apply it to our work. Sometimes in our striving we forget the part about actually getting to work. Trust God for the results. Spending undue amounts of time worrying over each decision to be made, looking for the perfect outcome and relying on everyone else to decide for you rather than making up your mind yourself will not help you avoid regret.

Also realize that trying to satisfy every person with an opinion on your wedding is not the same as being unselfish. Accepting input graciously is important. Changing your mind with every new piece of input is not really being unselfish. It can be another form of selfishness to make everyone scurry to accommodate a new plan because you've changed your mind *again* as you try to make everyone happy with you. Being kind and gracious is the goal, not making everyone happy.

A gracious woman of valor is both kind and productive. You can produce the wedding of your dreams without being selfish and demanding. It is not only okay, but a good thing to know what you want. There is no virtue in walking all over everyone to get your way. Nor is there virtue in being so accommodating that no decision is ever reached and no one can get anything done. If you treat others well in producing what you want, the result will be a wedding that is just what you dreamed of and which everyone involved has found joy in creating. Consider what kind of bride you are and how *you* can best serve others. You may not be so tempted to be demanding. You may need to choose to be more decisive.

If a little self-evaluation leads you to think that your struggle will be more on the being decisive end of things, here are a few thoughts to help you do well as a bride.

Choose one or two people whose taste and wisdom you trust. Ask them to be your go-to people for wedding advice. Bounce your ideas and decisions off of them. Let their opinions guide you if you need help in making a final decision.

Limit your options. Don't try and choose from every available wedding dress—choose one or two shops to try out and decide from those options. If being decisive is hard for you, it may be more important to be able to make a choice than to have every option available.

Let someone you trust take over a particular piece of the planning. If you have someone you trust with similar taste who is willing to take over a piece of the wedding, then that will relieve some of the pressure. You must then simply choose to be happy with whatever they produce. Take your hands off that portion of the wedding and let them do something creative and beautiful for you. Sometimes it is easy to be happy with something someone has done for you when you would be pickier about doing it yourself.

Let your fiancé be your guard. Sometimes there is a particular person in your life who you feel extra pressure to keep happy. When they give opinions or make comments about your choices, you worry there is going to be conflict or emotional upheaval. Displeasing them is especially worrisome and upsetting to you. When this is the case, use your fiancé as your guard and counselor. Let his judgment be the guide of whether to heed that person's input or disregard it. If there is potential conflict, let him handle the conversation. If need be, let him be the one to draw the line and decide whether it is best for you not to spend time with that person or discuss certain matters with them. It may be best to let him be the go-between when it is necessary to involve that person in the wedding, or at the very least have him present when that person is around. The Lord has given us protections and coverings for every difficulty. Your fiancé will soon be your covenant head. Now may be the time to start looking to him to be your defender and guide with emotionally difficult people in your life.

Lastly, being productive also means getting down to getting the work *done*. A bride of might, strength, and power will need **a willing determination to**

work hard. You may have a work schedule to keep up with, other duties to attend to, and commitments to fulfill. Adding a wedding into your schedule may be daunting. However, the wedding chores *have* to get done. Accepting this reality will help you successfully avoid wedding frustrations and disasters born of procrastination, dawdling, and flatly leaving the work for someone else to do. If you are going to get married on a particular date at a particular time, certain things have to happen. Tasks must be completed, steps taken towards an end goal. Be determined not to let yourself create excuses. Excise the words, "I'm tired!" from your vocabulary for the next few weeks or months. The mighty, strong woman of Proverbs 31 that we all aim to be chooses to work determinedly, sometimes in spite of weariness, emotions, conflicts, etc. A cheerful busyness and productive work ethic is every bride's best friend.

> *Give her of the fruit of her hands,*
> *and let her own works praise her in the gates.*
>
> (PROVERBS 31:31)

Capturing a Vision

RIGHT NOW YOU HAVE A VISION IN MIND. A VISION OF the perfect wedding. Lord willing, your wedding. You can see it all in your mind's eye, and all that is left is figuring out how to bring that vision to life. The picture in your head is what guides you through the many choices of colors and fabrics, candles and bouquets. It gives you direction when you are faced with an array of choices. Your vision is what keeps you working through the growing avalanche of wedding chores. Vision motivates.

As an engaged couple, there is another vision I encourage you to capture. This picture is of a home and family, a mission, a goal, an inheritance to pass on to children's children. Just as your vision of the perfect wedding drives you to create it in reality, choose to spend some time together capturing a vision of the family you want to create. Make it a grand, high, and full vision. Let life pour out of this picture of what your home and family will represent and the mission you will embrace.

In the midst of enjoying your love and anticipating your wedding day, find time together to create this vision of who you want to be as one. A vision is only that—a view of what the best possibility would look like. Of course, God works all kinds of unexpected mysteries into our lives, and our visions seldom look like the reality we arrive at. The purpose of creating this vision of your lives as one in Christ is not to institute a list of expectations of what *has to happen* in order for you to feel happy and successful. Rather, having a vision for yourself as a wife and together as a family produces a sense of purpose and goals to strive for in your early years of home building. Proverbs 14:1 tells us a wise woman builds her house. Vision helps us be good builders.

As *Pilgrim's Progress* so aptly pictured for us, traveling life's path together will bring many unexpected bends and switchbacks that could cause you to lose sight of your vision or goal in the distance. However, knowing that vision is there will help keep you on the path, rather than wallowing in the ditches. It is easy to get distracted or to forget the *goal* of the day-to-day busyness and labor that fill your life. Having set out with a vision for where you are going with all these efforts will give you perseverance for the tasks at hand, from folding laundry to buying a home.

Keeping your eyes on the prize (Philippians 3:14) will guard you from discouragement and weariness when your current circumstances become difficult. Our calling in Christ Jesus is our ultimate prize for which we strive. However, applying that calling in Christ to our family calling gives us missional work to do in our homes every day.

Use part of this engagement time to set goals and ideas for who you want to be as a couple, what you want your family to look like, and what mission you are striving for in Christ together. Then you will have a point of reference to come back to as the circumstances of life ebb, flow, and change direction. Choose a path together now that you will work to stay on, striving together to reach that "heavenly city."

When my husband and I were getting together, we had several unusual circumstances. These circumstances led many around us to be concerned about the wisdom of our relationship. In order to address these concerns, we did much talking and even wrote out a vision for our relationship and our instant family (my husband had five children from a previous marriage). Every few years on our anniversary, I take out those lists and papers and reread them. Much of what we envisioned and the goals we set did not end up applying at all. Many things changed as our family developed over the years. However, those goals and vision for our family were good. They helped set us in a positive direction and encouraged us to be purposeful in ministering to our children, our church, and our community through our marriage. I believe we were much better for having started out with a vision of what we wanted our family to be.

What else does a family vision accomplish? It inspires you to reach high. Even if you do not fulfill every aspect of your family vision, you will probably do more for having striven for great heights. Your wedding day is a mountain-peak high. Not every day will be such an exhilarating experience. Many days you have to trudge, rather than feeling as if you can fly. A vision towards which you travel will help motivate you to keep trudging on. A shared vision of your life as a family helps build unity and loyalty between you, and helps you avoid all those potential little pitfalls of newly married life. Which way *is* that silly roll of toilet paper supposed to go after all?! With a unified vision, together you will learn to share the same priorities, work towards similar ends, and be on the same page as you set up your home and family style.

The next time you and your fiancé are walking together, enjoying dinner out, or sitting around chatting, dreaming of your wedding day, spend a few moments dreaming a good vision of your life together. And don't just dream. Seriously discuss a unified vision for your family's mission for Christ in the world. Then pursue your vision with joy, in submission to Christ and one

another, and see what work God unfolds through this
new family He has created!

For I know the thoughts that I think toward you, says the Lord,
thoughts of peace and not of evil, to
give you a future and a hope.

(JEREMIAH 29:11)

Girlfriends

*Then the kingdom of heaven shall be likened to ten virgins
who took their lamps and went out to meet the bridegroom.
Now five of them were wise, and five were foolish.*

(MATTHEW 25:1–2)

*The royal daughter is all glorious within the palace; her
clothing is woven with gold. She shall be brought to the King
in robes of many colors; the virgins, her companions who
follow her, shall be brought to You. With gladness and rejoicing
they shall be brought; they shall enter the King's palace.*

(PSALM 45:13–15)

GIRLFRIENDS ARE SUCH A BLESSING. THEY GIGGLE OVER
your romance, provide shoulders to cry on in your
disappointments, cheer when you show up with a ring
on your finger, and hold your hand when you hyper-
ventilate over the price of wedding dresses. Having
your best girlfriends surrounding you as you enjoy the

time of being a bride makes the experience more memorable. They make you feel good about how great you
are going to look, talk you through your fears and inse-
curities, buy you lacy lingerie, and tease your fiancé
about what a great catch he's getting. Getting married
just wouldn't be the same without bridesmaids.

Choosing those bridesmaids can be a bit tricky.
Which of your girlfriends is maid of honor material?
What politics are involved in who is included and who
is left out? Who will make wedding events fun and
memorable, and who will just bring you down? Who
will help you arrive blessed and lovely at the end of
the aisle, and who might contribute to the stress of the
day? Who will you still be likely to know twenty years
from now? You may have had your bridesmaids picked
out since you were four, or you may be at a loss to find
any suitable girlfriends at all. Either way, sometimes
choosing attendants can be a bit of a pickle.

As with all such wedding pickles, wisdom is in
order. What does wisdom have to say in this matter?
*"And the second, like it, is this: 'You shall love your neighbor as
yourself.' There is no other commandment greater than these"*
(Mark 12:3).

Being included in someone's wedding is a privilege
and delight. It is also a great responsibility and sometimes requires great cost. Wisdom calls you to be loving
in your choice of wedding attendants. It means loving
your mother, mother-in-law, groom, sisters, brothers,

cousins, and friends more than you love your own style, vision, and desires for your wedding day.

Be loving, both when choosing on whom to bestow this honor, and in what you require of them. Loving your neighbor may mean taking into account who your mother or mother-in-law hopes you will include in the wedding. It may mean having more or fewer bridesmaids than you imagined. Love may require you to leave out someone in order to spare her a greater financial or time burden than she can bear. Loving your neighbor may mean changing the date to allow a particular person to participate. It may ask you to consider altering the style of the wedding for the sake of what your loved one can afford to buy or feels comfortable wearing. Is it more important to have the wedding "just so" or to make a way to include particular people in your wedding party? Blessings fall down in abundance on those who sacrifice self in love for another. What choices can you make that will be a blessing?

Wisdom also calls for a bride to surround herself with bridesmaids who will make her better. Choose wise virgins, not foolish ones. Do you have certain friends who tempt you to gossip about your future husband or constantly demean him or marriage in front you? Do you have certain girlfriends who always inspire you to be at your best or encourage you away from temptations toward besetting sins, complaining, or dissatisfaction? Usually we have friends who calm us and help us relax and other friends who are more work and often add to our stress load. While love may require including people who are not easy in your wedding party, when possible, consider which friends will aid you in being a blessing as a bride.

Wisdom also calls you to practice being a wise woman as you interact with your bridesmaids in the coming weeks. Heed the encouragements from that book of wisdom, Proverbs:

> *The lips of the righteous feed many, but*
> *fools die for lack of wisdom.*
>
> (PROVERBS 10:21)

> *She opens her mouth with wisdom, and on*
> *her tongue is the law of kindness.*
>
> (PROVERBS 31:26)

> *The wise woman builds her house, but the*
> *foolish pulls it down with her hands.*
>
> (PROVERBS 14:1)

Begin building your house in wisdom now by speaking carefully with your girlfriends about your husband-to-be and the wedding. Be discreet and chaste when you discuss your fiancé and your honeymoon with them. Be careful not to over-share his mistakes and faults. You and he are both learning relationship skills. Don't you hope he doesn't share your slip-ups and failures with his friends? Guard him from shame and ridicule by how you speak of him to others. Build his reputation and his glory. Remember again that you are his glory (1 Corinthians 11:7). Bore all your girlfriends with the wonders of your love rather than ever tantalizing them with even one juicy story of how he made a fool of himself with you.

Delight in your girlfriends and this particularly girlishly fun slice of life. Have lovely outings with your bridesmaids, picking out dresses and having your nails done. Get their advice on how to look your best and how to best please your man. Spend hours discussing the minutiae of wedding style with them, rather than with a future husband who probably just doesn't understand what makes minutiae interesting. Enjoy all this bridal time, beginning with choosing your wedding "virgins" wisely and ending with behaving wisely in their company.

Honoring Marriage

*Marriage is honorable among all, and the bed undefiled;
but fornicators and adulterers God will judge.*

(HEBREWS 13:4)

JUST A LITTLE REMINDER, IN CASE YOU MIGHT HAVE FORgotten in the midst of dress fittings and caterer interviews: you are getting married!

By this act alone you are waging warfare on our current American culture. Even a short perusal of college campuses, cable television, Supreme Court cases, and even many evangelical churches leads to the conclusion that marriage is no longer honorable among *many*. The very idea of marriage is ridiculed and attacked by those working to promote homosexuality, promiscuity, easy no-fault divorce, abortion, pornography, and more. The founding principle of much of American advertising is "sex sells." Outside of Christian circles it has become poor judgment and lack of wisdom to even consider marrying someone before "testing the waters" of your relationship by living together. Increasingly, the validity or purpose of going through the motions of getting married is being questioned in a world of readily available divorce and live-in boyfriends. Choosing monogamous, heterosexual marriage is an act of defiance against a progressively God-hating, anti-Christian culture. Well done! Your very wedding day is a victory shout for the army of God.

Because we are at such open war with worldliness in our culture today, promoting the honor of marriage is an ever more crucial part of our Christian testimony. Living in our marriages with honor speaks the truth of Christ to a world that derides and defames marriage. The Bible sets forth marriage as God's picture to the world of the relationship between Christ and His Church (2 Corinthians 10:2; Ephesians 5:22-33; Revelation 19:2-9, 21). We want our marriages to image that relationship correctly and thus speak the truth of Christ to the world. We live our marriages in the world, but our marriages are not of the world (Romans 12:2, 2 Corinthians 6:14-17, 1 John 2:15-17). **Christian marriage should look different.** Embrace marriage as your warfare with the world and the devil.

What can you do now, while yet a bride, to prepare to live this kind of antithetical marriage? In this chapter, I would like to focus on one of the most important aspects of transforming our current culture's view of marriage.

Honor your marriage bed.

To begin with, choose chastity now while you are engaged. The closer you get to your marriage bed, the harder it becomes to wait for it. It grows very tempting to say, "Well, we'll be married soon anyway." Your particular choices about dating and courtship may or may not include physical protections. However, be aware that the temptations you face are stronger than you will expect, and your resistance is weaker than you think. Place guards around yourself and make wise choices about what you do and where you go together. Flee temptation—don't try and walk a fine line. Christian churches are full of young couples that didn't quite "make it" to their honeymoon. Live antithetically to our culture even before you are married, and wait to consummate your relationship until it is a *marriage* relationship.

On the other hand, *do* prepare your heart and mind to take joy in your marriage bed. The wisdom literature of the Bible repeatedly tells a man to delight in his own wife and her alone. As wives, it is our job to be delightful. Sometimes, in working so diligently at chastity before marriage, a young woman can neglect to prepare herself for a healthy sexual life after marriage. "With my body I thee serve" is a phrase which has been removed from most wedding vows today because of how scandalous it is to the modern listener. Serving one another in love is a scandal to a world that tells you to insist on your rights. Just as serving one another in your day-to-day life together will build your marriage, so will it be in your physical relationship. Your body is no longer your own after you wedding day (I Corinthians 7:4). Preparing to use the physical gifts God has given you to bring joy to your husband is a way to honor your marriage bed.

Discovery is a joyful aspect of the honeymoon. Taking a few preparatory steps will make this time of discovery more enjoyable for you and your husband. If possible, schedule an appointment with your O.B.G.Y.N. before the wedding. Ask her to fill you in on any peculiarities you should be aware of about your body and what preparations you can make to facilitate your comfort and health during your honeymoon. Talk to a trusted older Christian woman or read a recommended Christian book that discusses the physical marital relationship. Seek to gain understanding of how your man is going to think of your sexual life. Learn about the differences between how you and he will think of this aspect of your relationship. There are several useful Christian books for engaged couples on preparing for the marriage bed. Ed Wheat's *Intended for Pleasure* is what my pastor husband always recommends in his premarital counseling sessions. I appreciate that it includes wise advice for a young woman about how to physically prepare for her wedding night.

Your pastor may also be able to suggest other useful resources during your premarital counseling sessions.

Another way we honor our marriage bed is to bring full and final resolution to any past relationships. Let there be no one even hoping to show up at your wedding proclaiming, "I object!" Let there be no corner of your own heart where a past relationship lingers. Whether you need to resolve to yourself or with another person, be clear that you belong to just one man now. There is no room for anyone else. Whatever baggage or scars you may carry from a previous relationship, be open with your husband. Let them be a part of your past that has formed you for him. Do not let there be someone lingering in the background, hoping your marriage will fail. Do not let a "backup" person linger in your heart in case that happens. Be your beloved's and let him belong to you.

Lastly, plan for your wedding *night* when you are planning your wedding. Time the wedding and honeymoon flights or any long drives in such a way that you won't be exhausted by the time you reach your wedding night. Arriving after midnight to your hotel or an early morning flight to Hawaii the next day may not be the best choice when considering delighting in your wedding night.

While you are busy choosing invitations and checking off guest lists, I invite you to commit yourself today to honoring marriage by how you live as a bride and a wife. Keep all these things in balance. Prepare to rejoice in your marriage bed, yet wait patiently for it. Consider how you may delight your husband, but keep these considerations close to the end of your engagement so as not to "stir up or awaken love too soon" (Song of Songs 2:7, 3:5, 8:4). Above all, reject the world's view of sexuality and live transformationally in your role as one man's woman. Honor your marriage, and let your bed be undefiled.

Gracious Beauty

A gracious woman retains honor, but ruthless men retain riches.

(Proverbs 11:16)

SO MANY OF US HAVE ONE IN OUR CLOSET. THAT DRESS. That dress you agreed to wear because you loved your friend and didn't want to be The Pain in her bridal party. You would never be caught dead wearing this dress in public of your own accord. Nothing but true friendship would compel you to leave the house in that color, ridiculous style, with that much bare flesh hanging out, or whatever the objection may be. Yet there it hangs, in the back of your closet. Why? Because it cost so darn much you can't bear to really admit that Goodwill is the only proper destination for it! Maybe there will be some reason to wear it again one day, right?

If you've ever been a bridesmaid yourself, you may well be able to relate to this experience of spending hundreds of dollars on a dress worn only once, feeling uncomfortable and unattractive the whole time you are wearing it. It is loving, gracious friendship that fills many a girl's closet with these nuisances. As the bride, it is up to you to exercise enough loving graciousness in the other direction to save your girlfriends from joining the ranks of expensive "hanger-decoration" owners!

The choosing of apparel can be the most difficult moment in working with your wedding party. A gracious spirit will go a long way towards creating an atmosphere of compromise and peace. Remember that the bride sets the tone. If you are gracious to your bridesmaids, groomsmen, and parents of flower girls and ring bearers, they are much more likely to be cooperative and anxious to please. If you demonstrate a desire to be considerate of the money they will need to spend to participate in your wedding, their gratitude will make them look more favorably on your final choices. Finding something you feel is beautiful and sets the right style for the wedding does not need to be at odds with pleasing those who will be wearing your choices.

What can you do to bring both the beauty of style and of a gracious spirit to your wedding party? A gracious bride pursues flexible options to avoid causing her bridesmaids to own expensive, unwearable burdens. She considers the expense she is asking of those participating in the wedding. Graciousness finds out the bridesmaids' individual comfort levels with strapless, backless and other possibly uncomfortable dress styles rather than waiting for someone to object. A gracious demeanor asks the groom what he prefers to wear or what colors he likes for the groomsmen's vests rather than simply informing him how it is going to be. A gracious bride holds her tongue and her temper when her best girlfriend turns on every finicky tendency she has. A gracious bride retains honor.

Graciousness can be extended in many ways during your wedding planning season beyond choosing bridal party apparel. *Gracious* as it is used in the Proverb denotes favor freely given. Can you imagine those who might covet your favor right now? Who would love to be freely given good standing in your eyes? I would imagine your new mother-in-law hopes to find favor in your sight. What can you do to put her at ease? In what way can you assure her that not only are you *not* stealing her son away, but you are anxious and pleased to become a part of his family? During the course of engagement events, you may meet many of your fiancé's relatives and previously unknown friends. These people who have known him all his life will also hope to discover that you welcome them freely. Extend yourself graciously to your new husband's family and friends. Take time to get to know them, make conversation, and listen attentively as they tell you their stories. Show yourself anxious to learn their ways and who they are. These people who also cherish your fiancé will rest easy and rejoice in the wonderful catch their grandson, nephew, cousin, or friend has found. Favor freely given will bring you honor in many of your new husband's circles.

Graciousness is an adornment that beautifies any woman. It turns a plain bride into a stunning beauty. Graciousness from the bride gives new eyes to the friends and family receiving her grace. They no longer see little flaws or failings. Instead, eyes of gratefulness and relief see a woman who is regal and refined, beautiful because of the fine spirit she carries. Graciousness bestows beauty on the bearer. The beautiful Vashti in the book of Esther brings humiliation on herself, her husband, and her kingdom by her graceless insistence on her own way. Esther, through her gracious speech and behavior towards the king (Esther 5-7) gains great honor and brings, "light and gladness, joy and honor" to her people (Esther 8:16). Bring light and gladness, joy and honor to your wedding day by treating those participating in your wedding with gracious lovingkindness.

Memory Keeper

Mary kept all these things, and pondered them in her heart.

(LUKE 2:19)

WHERE? WHEN? HOW? THESE ARE QUESTIONS WE are taught to ask from our earliest years. Right now your big questions are: "Where and when will this wedding be held?" and, "How are we going to pull this off?!" There are a lot of questions in the journey of our lives. "Mommy, *how* did you and Daddy first meet? *When* did you know Daddy was the one for you? *Where* did you get married?" The when, where, and how's of life form our memories, our story.

Now is the time to treasure up these story-building memories. In most cases, women are the memory keepers for the family. We are the ones who make the scrapbooks, keep the baby journals, and answer the when, where, and how's of life for our children. We treasure up the family vacations, weddings, funerals, births, moving days, new places, and good-byes to old places that create our family's story. We are the keepers of the memories. Your family's story begins now, with your engagement and wedding day. It is time for you to begin being the memory keeper.

Luke tells us that Jesus' mother was a memory keeper. She observed all the amazing events surrounding her child's birth and young life and, "kept all these things, and pondered them in her heart." Mary is an excellent example for us. We should ponder the Lord's work in our lives. Notice the great acts He does on your behalf. The day-to-day miracles of our lives may not seem so miraculous. However, if we have eyes to see, His hand is at work everywhere in and through us. Recognize the little miracles of your life and ponder them. Treasure them up. These form the story of our lives. These are the moments our children will want to hear about one day. Pondering them in your heart and mind is how you become the keeper of your family's story.

Psalm 78:4 says, "We will not hide them from their children, telling to the generation to come the praises of the Lord, and His strength and His wonderful works that He has done." **This is our job: to tell our children the wonderful works God has done in our lives.** However, we cannot tell what we have not even noticed ourselves. I encourage you to take the time to notice, appreciate, and remember the wonderful works of God as they are happening in your life. Everyone has a love story. Consider what moments you are experiencing now which will form the love story that you will tell your children.

How can you reveal the glory of God to little eyes by the way you keep and tell about the memories of these days? I enjoy watching the movie, *The Prize Winner of Defiance, Ohio.* It is a true story created from the memoirs of one child in a family of twelve. Because of her mother, this daughter was able to see their obviously sad and discouraging home life in a uniquely blessed and positive way, despite her drunken failure of a father. Her mother, by choosing to turn what would otherwise be the ugly parts of life into thankful, cheerful memories, presented a family story to her children of hope and joy rather than suffering and bitterness. Watching this funny and heart-breaking movie always reminds me that the *way* you keep your family story can communicate the grace and glory of God to future generations. What kind of memory keeper you will be is something to consider as you set out on your family story.

Some people are natural born storytellers. They will remember all kinds of wonderful things in their lives and tell them as captivating stories for years. Others of us need things like journals and scrapbooks to help us tell our stories. A good beginning is just learning to ponder. As your new family's story begins, ponder the wonderful works that God is doing in you. Then consider how you will share them.

If you are not a natural storyteller, what can you do to remember the bits of your story that your children will be asking about one day? You may want to start a wedding memories journal and take the time to keep it. Maybe it is more your style to take tons of photographs and make a scrapbook of your courtship and engagement. Another option is to maintain a wedding blog and have both you and your fiancé's versions of your love story on it. Many of the great stories of history have been preserved in letters exchanged at the time and kept to be discovered later by children or historians. Writing letters is fast becoming a lost art. The blog is one of the new ways of story keeping that is replacing letter-writing. I know many young women who keep a family blog and post to it regularly so that family and friends can share in their family story. Maybe this would be what works best for you. If storytelling is not your forté, consider what way you can learn to preserve your family memories.

Choose a method of memory-keeping that you will enjoy and actually keep up. A good story is one told by a person who delights in the telling. Memory-keeping should not be something you dread or carry around as a guilty weight because you are so behind in it. I certainly do not want to add to your load of chores during this busy wedding season! I encourage you to find the way you best love to tell your story and to pursue it. Be the memory keeper for your family so that years from now the next generation may hear of it and glorify God in you.

Building Your Storehouse

I LOVE THE STORY OF ABIGAIL. THERE IS MUCH TO ENJOY IN it—the courage of this wife, how she lays down her pride and takes her husband's sin upon herself, the tension and excitement of her race to deliver her household from David's wrath. It's just a good *story*. It is also full of treasures for inspiring us to greater glory as women of God. Today, as you contemplate your coming role as a valorous wife of priceless value (Proverbs 31:10), I want to draw your attention to one particular point in this story.

> *Now one of the young men told Abigail, Nabal's wife, saying, "Look, David sent messengers from the wilderness to greet our master; and he reviled them. But the men were very good to us, and we were not hurt, nor did we miss anything as long as*

we accompanied them, when we were in the fields. They were a wall to us both by night and day, all the time we were with them keeping the sheep. Now therefore, know and consider what you will do, for harm is determined against our master and against all his household. For he is such a scoundrel that one cannot speak to him."

Then Abigail made haste and took two hundred loaves of bread, two skins of wine, five sheep already dressed, five seahs of roasted grain, one hundred clusters of raisins, and two hundred cakes of figs, and loaded them on donkeys. And she said to her servants, "Go on before me; see, I am coming after you." *But she did not tell her husband Nabal. So it was, as she rode on the donkey, that she went down under cover of the hill; and there were David and his men, coming down toward her, and she met them.*

Now David had said, "Surely in vain I have protected all that this fellow has in the wilderness, so that nothing was missed of all that belongs to him. And he has repaid me evil for good. May God do so, and more also, to the enemies of David, if I leave one male of all who belong to him by morning light."

Now when Abigail saw David, she dismounted quickly from the donkey, fell on her face before David, and bowed down to the ground. So she fell at his feet

and said: "On me, my lord, on me let this iniq-
uity be! And please let your maidservant speak in
your ears, and hear the words of your maidservant.
Please, let not my lord regard this scoundrel Nabal.
For as his name is, so is he: Nabal is his name, and
folly is with him! But I, your maidservant, did not
see the young men of my lord whom you sent. Now
therefore, my lord, as the Lord lives and as your
soul lives, since the Lord has held you back from
coming to bloodshed and from avenging yourself
with your own hand, now then, let your enemies
and those who seek harm for my lord be as Nabal.
And now this present which your maidservant has
brought to my lord, let it be given to the young men
who follow my lord. Please forgive the trespass of
your maidservant. For the Lord will certainly make
for my lord an enduring house, because my lord
fights the battles of the Lord, and evil is not found
in you throughout your days. Yet a man has risen
to pursue you and seek your life, but the life of my
lord shall be bound in the bundle of the living with
the Lord your God; and the lives of your enemies He
shall sling out, as from the pocket of a sling. And it
shall come to pass, when the Lord has done for my
lord according to all the good that He has spoken
concerning you, and has appointed you ruler over
Israel, that this will be no grief to you, nor offense
of heart to my lord, either that you have shed blood

*without cause, or that my lord has avenged himself.
But when the Lord has dealt well with my lord, then
remember your maidservant."*

*Then David said to Abigail: "Blessed is the Lord
God of Israel, who sent you this day to meet me! And
blessed is your advice and blessed are you, because
you have kept me this day from coming to bloodshed
and from avenging myself with my own hand. For
indeed, as the Lord God of Israel lives, who has kept
me back from hurting you, **unless you had hurried
and come to meet me**, surely by morning light no
males would have been left to Nabal!"*

*So David received from her hand what she
had brought him, and said to her, "Go up in peace
to your house. See, I have heeded your voice and
respected your person."* (1 Samuel 25:14–35,
emphasis added)

Abigail responds immediately to the news that
David and his mighty men are coming to punish
her husband and destroy her household. She is only
able to accomplish what she does because she has
great resources at hand. How could she bring gifts
and appease David if she hadn't had storehouses of
resources, readily available, from which to take bread,
wine, and cakes? How would she have gotten to him
if she didn't have donkeys on which to carry these

appeasements and servants to help her act quickly?
There is no pause in the story. Abigail hears the words
of the young man and acts immediately to gather these
tributes and go to David.

I encourage you, as a bride looking forward to
taking on the role of wife, to start building up your
storehouse of resources now. You will be faced with
many situations over the years—trials, emergencies,
or the needs of others—when you will find yourself
needing to respond *well*, immediately. There will not
always be time to gather the strength, wisdom, advice,
or help. If you have built up a good supply of these
assets in your "storehouse," you will be much more
ready to respond quickly and correctly the moment a
crisis arrives at your doorstep.

So, this raises the question, what resources best
sustain a woman of God? Here are a few ideas to get
you started:

Devote yourself to the Word of God and prayer.
A well-fed soul is the greatest resource you can have.
A skinny soul dies quickly when famine arrives. A fat
soul can outlast a period of starvation. Feed your soul
during your times of feasting and joy so that you will
be ready when times of fasting and trial come.

Gather wise women about you. So often *perspective*

is what sets us off on the wrong track in response to trials or bad attitudes. We lose perspective and blow things out of proportion or tell ourselves the wrong story about what is really happening in our lives. Wise woman counselors help bring godly perspective to our lives. Don't wait for the trial to come to seek help. Start learning and gleaning from the godly women in your life now. Visit with them. Hang out with them. Go to their homes and serve them in some way. I have learned most of what is best in my life through working with other, better women and learning from them as we work.

If you are not blessed with local women to befriend, **use the tools of Internet, books, and audio resources** readily available almost everywhere now. Even if you do know wonderful Christian women in person, it can be useful to learn from the examples of others as well. Find homemaking blogs written by women who love their homes and families. Read books, both instructive (e.g., the works of Nancy Wilson) and exemplary (e.g., biographies of Christian women).

Listen to books on CD if you don't have the time to read. I can't tell you how many profitable works I've listened to while doing my dishes! Listen to sermons or talks on godly womanhood. Learning from real flesh-and-blood women is best, but don't let their absence discourage you. We can store up wisdom from other godly women in many ways. Here is a small sampling of some resources I've enjoyed:

- www.feminagirls.com
- http://journeychronicles.blogspot.com
- http://www.doorposts.com/blog/
- *Evidence Not Seen,* by Darlene Deibler Rose
- *Kitty, My Rib,* by E. Jane Mall
- *A Chance to Die,* and other books by Elizabeth Elliot
- *Disciplines of a Godly Woman,* by Barbara Hughes
- *The Fruit of Her Hands,* and other books by Nancy Wilson
- *The Pleasant Home,* and other audio sets by Nancy Wilson

Make room in your life to **acquire new skills**. Buy a good cookbook with lots of instructions. My culinary life changed when I checked out *The Pie and Pastry Bible* from the library and read it one summer. Buy a good camera and learn how to use it. Take up gardening or sewing. Study the history of some particular place or time period. The Proverbs 31 woman is a lady of many talents and abilities that she has clearly developed over time. The more capable, knowledgeable, and skilled you make yourself, the better wife you will be.

Attend a Bible study. Keep yourself growing not only in your personal study of the Word, but in the company others. "As iron sharpens iron, so a man sharpens the countenance of his friend" (Proverbs 27:17). Your knowledge of the Word grows in different ways when you study it with others.

Build up and be a good steward of physical resources. Engagement is the perfect time to start a hope chest, even if you haven't grown up with one. Whether you have a physical hope chest or not, you can pursue the concept of collecting physical resources for your coming role as wife. Gather items for your home that will enable you to make it a center of hospitality and service to your husband, family, and community. What talents do you have that can benefit your future family? Invest in the tools that will help you put those talents to good use. For example, if you love cooking, stock your hope chest with quality knives, fine cookware, etc. While you are still single, your income may be less encumbered by bills, the costs of raising a family, etc., than later in life. Use this opportunity to stock up on quality tools for the future.

Start a piggy bank. Money is a resource that gives you the freedom to bless your future family in many ways. Two stories that inspired me along these lines were the old movie, *The Glen Miller Story,* and a book called *A Tree Grows in Brooklyn.* Glen Miller's wife was able to hand him the money to start his big band from the change she had been saving from his pockets throughout their marriage. The poor, tenement slum mother in turn-of-the-century Brooklyn had the vision of bettering her family by purchasing a home. She saved her pennies, nickels, and dimes to that end in a tin can bank, nailed to the closet floor.

Having a piggy-bank savings mentality cultivates the self-control of being a wise steward of all the money that passes through your hands. It also gives you the resources to do special things for your loved ones. I was able to take my daughter to New York City for her sixteenth birthday partly by saving my pop can recycling money, spare change, and leftover grocery money for a few years.

Bringing money into a marriage is another way to bless your future husband. Do your best to pay off any debts you have now, before the wedding, and to save as much as possible leading up to your marriage. Both as a bride and a wife, bless your husband and family by being a good steward of money.

Whichever of these ideas suit your circumstances and personality, the goal is to start your own "storehouse" of resources. Be a mighty woman of valor like Abigail—ready to act in a time of need. Have the mindset of looking forward by acting now in a way that will make you strong, useful, and prepared for the future. How can you build *your* storehouse?

Rejoicing in the Lord

Rejoice in the Lord always. Again I will say, rejoice!

"A T THE END OF THE DAY WE'LL BE MARRIED." THAT'S
what my husband kept repeating to me throughout
our engagement. Whenever I got stressed out about
what we couldn't afford, what detail was falling through,
or all that might go wrong, he would repeat that to me.
It reminded us both that, ultimately, none of what hap-
pened, or didn't happen perfectly, on our wedding day
really mattered to us except that we would finally and
truly be married to each other.

That's how I knew, when he came knocking at my
dressing room door and spoke those words through a
crack in the doorway, that something was wrong. Those
words were our motto against getting freaked out over
whatever might happen on the wedding day. If he was
saying those words now, something was going wrong.

As it turned out, the florist had arrived several hours late with the wrong number and kinds of arrangements. Our pastor's wife came to the rescue, went to a local floral stand and filled in our arrangements. All was well. A spider crawled out of my bouquet during the ceremony and got smashed all over my dress, ruining it for later use, but we were too busy rejoicing in finally *being married* to care.

Rejoicing in everything allows little things like green spider stains to be funny stories you tell your friends later instead of occasions for bitter regret. A rejoicing spirit takes calmly what a fearful or perfectionistic spirit will find a major crisis. A heart full of rejoicing doesn't even see the little things that are not "just-so" on the wedding day.

It may be hard to imagine that you would be anything but filled with rejoicing on your wedding day. However, that depends on your spirit now. Like all spiritual disciplines, a heart of rejoicing requires practice and cultivation. If you are not rejoicing all along the way, then you will not have trained your eyes to look on the events of the day in a way that sees the things to rejoice in. Are you continually stressing out over the many little decisions that come with wedding planning? Then you are likely to still be stressing out as you watch your wedding plans unfold on the day. A heart of rejoicing has to be cultivated. It doesn't simply switch on when you walk down the aisle. A rejoicing heart looks down that aisle to the man standing there, eagerly waiting to marry you. A fearful, anxiety-driven heart looks at the veil and bouquet and pew bows and worries about whether they turned out just right or not.

If you are prone to be a worrier, how can you cultivate this heart of rejoicing? How can you develop the ability to relax and rejoice in your wedding day?

We hold wedding feasts because our family and friends have gathered from near and far. They are rejoicing with us over the Lord's work in establishing our marriage. Feasting is evidence of rejoicing hearts. To help cultivate your rejoicing heart, feast before the Lord. Feast on the beauty you find as you pull together fabrics, ribbons, and flowers. Feast on the rich joys presented to you as you watch your mother, sisters, or girlfriends delight in your wedding plans. Feast on the outpouring of love you receive from your friends and families at bridal showers and engagement parties. Feast on the pleasure of waking up each morning, one day closer to marrying the man you love. Indulge yourself in your joy. Now is not the time for spiritual dieting. Gorge yourself on the love, praise, glory, and joy being poured upon you.

Jesus said, "Can the friends of the bridegroom fast while the bridegroom is with them? As long as they have the bridegroom with them, they cannot fast" (Mark 2:19, Luke 5:34, Matthew 9:15). How unthinkable to put on fasting and a heart of mourning during the time of bridal joy! Let your heart feast on all the little delights of being a bride, and on your wedding day you will have a heart overflowing with rejoicing.

Complaining kills joy. How was the Israelites' victorious joy, after escaping Egypt, killed? By complaining about the food and drink on the other side. How does a foolish woman tear down her house? With a complaining attitude and tongue (Proverbs 14:1, 21:9, 25:24). Complaining is a choice. Choose how you will approach the decisions you make for the wedding.

Finding fault all along the way in your wedding plans will kill your joy. If you choose to complain about the high cost, the uncooperative people, the unavailability of particular things you really wanted, you will find nothing to rejoice in on the wedding day either. However, if you rejoice in the many gifts God puts into your hand and call whatever He provides *good*, you will see the loveliness to rejoice in all along the way *and* on your wedding day. Suddenly, what you have will become just the right amount of money, just the right attendants, just the right family, just the right venue, and just the right good thing you hoped for. Look with eyes to see everything you receive as from the hand of God—good gifts of joy for you—and guard your heart and tongue from complaining.

Each morning as you rise, take a moment to rejoice in what the day holds. Rejoice in the exciting things you have planned and in the tasks you need to accomplish.

Rejoice that God has given both into your hands to do. Cultivate a heart of rejoicing that will make your wedding day a delight that carries forth into your new home.

Giving Good Gifts to Your Groom

*Who can find a virtuous wife? For her worth is
far above rubies. The heart of her husband safely
trusts her; so he will have no lack of gain.*

(PROVERBS 31:10-11)

*An excellent wife is the crown of her husband, but she
who causes shame is like rottenness in his bones.*

(PROVERBS 12:4)

*He who finds a wife finds a good thing, and
obtains favor from the Lord.*

(PROVERBS 18:22)

*Houses and riches are an inheritance from
fathers, but a prudent wife is from the Lord.*

(PROVERBS 19:14)

ISN'T THIS WHAT WE ALL LONG TO BE FOR OUR MEN? A
wife of such surpassing worth that everyone recognizes it and he counts you above riches and kingdoms.

Right now he may spend every other moment telling you and everyone you know how great you are. But deep down, don't we often wonder to ourselves, is it true? Are we really deserving of the praise our husbands (or husbands-to-be) bestow upon us?

There are two good gifts we can bestow upon our husbands that will make us wives who are worthy of such great acclaim. Proverbs tells us both. First, be so trustworthy that he rests assured you will only do him good all your days. Be trustworthy—faithful—loyal. Loyalty to your new husband makes you a wife to be treasured. Second, give him glory and not shame. Build him up by the way you act and speak towards him and about him. Just as we women thrive on attentive, cherishing love, our men thrive on our praise and glory. An excellent wife brings her husband glory.

First, we need to consider what womanly loyalty looks like. What new loyalties will come to you when you say, "I do," and how can you be preparing for them now? For starters, you are to be loyal to the Lord. After that, you are to be loyal to the husband the Lord is giving you. When you marry, your loyalties transfer from the family you have grown up in to the husband and new family you are creating. As his wife, you are his number one cheerleader. He always knows you are on his side. He is the one you defer to. He is the one you seek to bless in your thoughts, speech, and actions. As he hears you tell your friends how wonderful he is, he rests in the assurance that you are overlooking his faults. As you spend your money wisely, he trusts that his work and income are good enough for you. As you defer to his judgment and never belittle him with his failures, he knows you trust him to lead your family. There are many ways of using your speech and good works to bring rest to your husband, both as his wife and now as his bride.

Begin considering how to be a loyal bride by reading the ideas listed below. Meditate on these and consider what else you can do which will bless the particular man God has given you:*

Tell him how much you appreciate the work he does every day and how proud you are of his vocation.

Consider his needs and wishes above all others in wedding matters and everyday concerns.

Dwell on his godly traits and share them proudly

---

* The inspiration for this section and much of the substance of the content was gleaned from Nancy Wilson. Particularly her CD series *Grandmother's and Mothers-in-Law: On to the Next Thing* and a post on her Femina blog entitled "**A Respectful Wife**" helped form the ideas and suggestions found here. I am indebted to all of Nancy's work for her excellent analogies and her instructive advice and wisdom on walking well before the Lord in the many seasons of a woman's life.

with your girlfriends and families. Be righteously proud of the husband God is giving you. Let him hear you praise him to others.

Express verbally to him how blessed you feel to be getting him for a husband! Tell him specific reasons why he is so perfectly suited to be your husband. Express gratitude to him and gratitude to God for him.

Speak to him with the law of kindness on your tongue, showing deference even in your differences.

If he asks something of you, make it your first priority. Put his requests and needs before the demands of the wedding or your personal schedule.

Go to him first for counsel, or at the very least, second, after your parents. It may be a little tricky during your engagement as you are not fully under his leadership until the wedding day. Until then, you still have remaining responsibility towards your parents' leadership. However, you can certainly begin to show your loyalty to him by seeking his counsel above others.

Pray for him daily. Pray for your coming marriage and your growth together. Pray the Spirit will inspire in you a trustworthy loyalty towards your future husband.

Be quick to forgive and slow to anger.

Don't repeat your disagreements to others. Don't over-share his faults or failures. Let your speech give him rest that you will never shame him before others, especially your family and close girlfriends. If you find yourself with a relational situation in your marriage that you do not have the skills to negotiate wisely, find one wise counselor to consult. Choose someone who is able to be a part of the solution to your problem. Repeating marital struggles to a girlfriend, your mom, or anyone who is not able to be part of the solution is the fastest way to tear down your relationship rather than build it up. We are always tempted to share our troubles with those who will sympathize and tell us what we want to hear. Mom may be the best source of wisdom and guidance. However, she could just be the one person you know will say, "Poor baby!" and take up an offense on your behalf. Be wise about seeking counsel and guarded in your speech.

The more you succeed in these daily good works towards your husband-to-be, the greater his trust in you will grow. These godly habits will form a foundation for the excellent wife you hope to be for the man you love.

As you build your fiancé's trust, also consider how

to fulfill the second part of being his priceless treasure. How can you give your fiancé glory? Consider whom you are marrying. How good is God to bring you such a perfect man to be your friend, lover, leader, and companion! A wedding is great fun, but being married to him will be so much greater! What a privilege to be married and to build a life serving the Lord together with joy. A consideration of the joy you find in your Prince Charming will prepare your heart and tongue to pour glory upon him.

When it comes to planning the wedding, how you consider and treat your groom can very much affect whether he receives glory from you or feels marginalized and uncared for. You may happily rejoice to be marrying the man of your dreams. However, there is also the temptation to rejoice a bit less in involving this same man in creating your dream wedding. Part of that American wedding culture mentioned previously, which caters to the bride as the center of the wedding universe, is a slighting or even demeaning of the groom. A groom is to wear what the bride tells him to, make sure to secure a wedding license, and show up on time. That's it. Any possible input he would have into the wedding plans is often portrayed as inappropriate or pushy. A girl has every right to get her feelings hurt if her groom says the wrong thing about the colors she's chosen or music she wants, right?

In order to live counter-culturally as a bride and

bring glory to your groom, start with going back to the basics. Practice the Golden Rule. If he went off and rented a church without your permission, or even input, wouldn't you be furious? Show him the same courtesy. Just because he is not the bride does not mean he forfeits the right to hold any opinions or be considered when making wedding decisions. It is true that many grooms could care less what colors the bridesmaids wear or what flowers you carry. Others will care so much about making their brides happy, they willingly keep their opinions to themselves. However, it is more often the case that brides and their mothers like to think the groom doesn't care so that they can feel good about not asking.

Your groom can make many valuable contributions to the wedding plans, and the occasion will turn out better for having had his input, perspective, and sense of style. Who wants to place the man they love in the unenviable position of either giving up any wishes he has for his wedding day or displeasing his beloved bride? Not you. You want a wedding that reflects the taste, style, and dreams you both are contributing to this special day.

At the other end of the spectrum is the type of groom who truly is indifferent to the wedding. Brides faced with a groom who is only interested in talking about their future together after the wedding have to be careful not to take offense at this either. This bride may find it easy to see her groom's lack of excitement about wedding decisions as a disinterest in marrying her. She just wishes she could get even one preference out of him! If he truly does not care, do not take it personally. He wants you. He is not slighting you or demeaning what is important to you because he doesn't care what color the napkins are at the reception. There is a difference between not caring a whole lot about the wedding and not caring about getting married. If your groom is bored by wedding details, go to your mom, girlfriends, or other women who will love to talk over every tidbit with you and help you make good decisions. Don't expect your groom to be your maid of honor.

Keeping a good balance between these two extremes means learning who your groom is. Before you jump to any preconceived notions about what grooms are and are not supposed to be like or care about, consider the one groom in your wedding. What kinds of things does he care about? What would he like to be involved in? What would he prefer to be left out of? How can you both include him in ways that show you value his judgment above all others and yet not make demands of him that set him up to fail you? How can you give your groom glory in the wedding planning? Recognize who he is and be thankful for the man you're marrying rather than judging him by what you think a groom should be like.

Today, start being a good advertisement for

marriage by the way you love your future husband. Let your thoughts, words, and actions towards your fiancé reveal to the world how grand you find it to be entering a life of belonging to this wonderful man. Give him glory in the way you consider and include him in the wedding planning. Let him both trust in you and revel in the way you build him up. Let him wonder how he ever felt a whole person without you in his life. Be a glory and treasure to your future husband today.

Say Thank You

*For the Lord will comfort Zion, He will comfort all her waste
places; He will make her wilderness like Eden, and her desert
like the garden of the Lord; **joy and gladness will be
found in it, thanksgiving and the voice of melody.***

(ISAIAH 51:3, EMPHASIS ADDED)

WHAT IS LEFT? YOU ARE COMING TO THE END OF YOUR time as Bride. What more can you do to bless others in this role before you exchange it for the role of Wife? What more is there to say about the bride than what has been discussed in the previous chapters? In an early chapter we discussed the importance of thankfulness, and we will end here with it as well. The key to joy is thankfulness from beginning to end. Wrap your joy in thanksgiving and it will be well preserved. *Say thank you.*

Who do you need to thank as you come to the end of your life as a single person? Your parents who have sacrificed themselves day after day for you in so many ways to bring you to this point? A pastor or his wife who have counseled and mentored you and helped build the character that so attracted your fiancé? A best friend who encouraged you through difficult times that developed you into who you are today? No one arrives at the next chapter of their life without the help of specific people God sends their way. *Who do you need to thank?*

As you approach the final days before your wedding, I encourage you to take a few moments out of your week to personally thank important people in your life. This may not be true for every bride, but the person I most encourage you to express your love and appreciation for is *your mother*. Our mothers live the life of a woman of God before us. From them we learn all the little ways of living for the Lord. Mothers sacrifice for us our entire lives. By doing our dishes, washing our wounds, and forgoing a new dress so we could have a cute, new Easter outfit, Mom has shown in real and practical ways what Christ-likeness is. Much of who you will be as a wife is due to the example and influence of your mother. The obscure and laborious task of being a mother is one of the least appreciated.

So, when you are making a list of the fun things you'd like to do in the week leading up to your wedding, make a little room to take your mom out on a date. Treat her to a fun mother-daughter outing just as she has treated you so many times before. Tell her what you appreciate about her. Consider all the specific ways your mom has blessed you and how different you would be but for her, and then *tell* her these things. Express the ways you hope to be the kind of wife she has been. Bless her with thankfulness. It will be a good way to begin your life as a wife, blessing the one who has shown you how.

The day of exchanging Bride for Wife is fast approaching. As you are radiating a spirit of thankfulness, consider the people in your *coming* life as well. Your future in-laws have trained and raised their son, making him the perfect man for you. Just as there are many people to thank in your life, there are those in his life who have served him in ways that are going to bless you. Take the time to show your appreciation to those who have influenced and formed your husband-to-be. Think specifically of how his upbringing has formed him in ways that bless you, and tell your future in-laws about them. Be grateful for their work in his life, and express it. Verbally sharing your appreciation of their loving labors will build your relationship with your future family.

Above and throughout all, give thanks to the Lord who has done all these good works for you. I often find when I am most happy and busy, I am least consistent in pausing to give prayerful thanks to the One who is providing that happiness. Take time out for prayers of thanksgiving. Speak words of praise as each little joy comes your way. Take time to stop and meditate on the goodness of God at work in your life right now. Let the words of Psalm 103 be on your lips constantly in this joyful time of being a bride. "Bless the Lord, O my soul; and all that is within me, bless His holy name!"

Let thanksgiving be the hallmark of your joy. All the preparations, goals, attitudes, and godly habits you have striven for in your time as a bride will produce fruits of holiness and blessing in your future as you wrap them in thanksgiving. As you say your "I do's" and leave this time of bride-hood, carry with you the holy habit of giving thanks in all things, and you will be more able to accomplish all that you hope as a wife. God bless you on your wedding day. May you have much joy in it.

Behold, bless the Lord, all you servants of the Lord, who by night stand in the house of the Lord! Lift up your hands in the sanctuary, and bless the Lord.

The Lord who made heaven and earth bless you from Zion!

(PSALM 134:1–3, EMPHASIS ADDED)

CPSIA information can be obtained at www.ICGtesting.com
Printed in the USA
LVOW10s1955011214

416503LV00030B/1449/P

9 780983 671978